HA HA

Sundress Publications • Knoxville, TN

Editor: Erin Elizabeth Smith
erin@sundresspublications.com
http://www.sundresspublications.com

Colophon: This book is set in Hoefler Text and Apple SD
Gothic Neo.

Cover Design: Mary Ellen Knight

Book Design: Erin Elizabeth Smith

Book Interior Design: Jane Huffman and T.A. Noonan

HA HA HA THUMP
Amorak Huey

For Peter & Gretchen—

Thanks for your friendship & for supporting the book — I hope you like the poems.

Amorak Huey

9-9-2015

GLCL

THANK YOU

Thank you to my colleagues in the Writing Department at Grand Valley State University for their continuing support. Thanks to Chris Haven, W. Todd Kaneko, Amy McInnis, and Aaron Brossiet for all those Aprils. Thanks to the rest of the Poet's Choice gang, past and present: Dean Rader, Mark Schaub, Christina Olson, Jean Prokott, Brian Komei Dempster, Judy Halebsky, Ashley Cardona, Katie Cappello, Brian Clements, Mike Henry, and Ander Monson. Thanks to my poetry teachers: Nancy Eimers, William Olsen, Daneen Wardrop, Sandra Sprayberry, David Kirby, Bob Hicok, Jill Alexander Essbaum, and Mary Ruefle. Thank you to Traci Brimhall and Matthew Olzmann. And special thanks to Erin Elizabeth Smith and the good people at Sundress for believing in this book.

For Malcolm, Marilyn, and Silas, who gave me a place to start.
For Ellen, who gave me a place to land.
For Zoe-Kate and Eli, who keep me moving.

CONTENTS

WHAT HAPPENS AT THE BLOCK PARTY
STAYS AT THE BLOCK PARTY

WHAT GOES "HA HA HA THUMP"?

HOW A STORY ENDS IS HOW WE WILL REMEMBER IT

Nocturne: Interrogation

When did you know it would end as it did?

Ask me instead the difference between snow and sand.
Between wind and blood.

Describe the taste of the first lie.

The pebbled light of winter.
A body departing.
Salt and christening wine.

Did you ever love truly?

Do not mistake the empty page for violence.

Did you ever love, truly?

Language is a kind of hunger.
Do not mistake my silence for absence.

CONFESSIONS
& OTHER CRIMES

Ha Ha Ha Thump

The morning of the extravagant crime you awaken
clockradio-crazy purple-bloated foxhole-weary—

you feel excessively formal, though underdressed,
poorly put together. Sunlight wrenches a trough

through any possibility of changing your mind.
Your sutures ooze. Your accusers will cite

this very moment as if it could be isolated.
Getting out of bed is harder than falling in love.

The agenda has something do with violence,
something to do with empathy.

This place is a rental, they all are,
impermanence of jigsaw puzzle

or cake of soap in warm water.
The day flukes and slaps before you:

someone laughing his head off.

At the Midnight Garage Sale

Amid rows of unplugged clutter this woman's got no teeth
but her hand's down your pants, first time for everything,

she's asking why a good-looking guy like you
doesn't have a girlfriend. Streetlights hum & flicker,

your head spins, scabs peel, this is zombie movie, mess, message
in broken bottle. Your childhood of laughtrack & Loony Tune

leaves you with a long list of things you'll learn later aren't true.
You don't have to wait twenty minutes to jump in this water,

skeletons sink in the murk, smokestacks climb from shadow.
The trick to understanding the meaning of a scene

is to look for the light source. It's dark, it's bright,
it's flat, flight, fantastic—they're practically giving this shit away,

here's a basket of angel wings, milk carton of melted wax,
a hundred enormous wooden spoons. Shoes that never fit anyone,

dress pants, slivers of soap. Rope that smells of blood,
fifty pounds of ashes. Table after table. Tell her you came

for the card game, but the joker's on you, ha ha.
Pay up or bug out, first taste free, there's a highway over your head

& you left a warm bed for this? They'll accuse you
of skimming the surface, short-handing your true emotions,

but no one can say you didn't try. The problem
isn't feeling nothing, it's feeling everything.

The Breaking Point Is the Coordinate on the Strain-Strength Curve at the Moment of Rupture

You stumble your stories before me like sand. Your sadness is an ocean.
You say all flaws are forgivable if we get the ending right.

We do not like surprise—
        the femme fatale suddenly has a cock,
        everything that mattered was a dream—

we do not like coincidence.

What about the time I made out with my best friend's ex-girlfriend
        on his mother's bed
while he was down the street stealing the radio from her truck?

Or the time another girlfriend not my own was about to go down on me

and I said, "Are you sure this is OK?" and she stopped to say yes,
        which led to a conversation about guilt
and the blow job became an afterthought.

You say, "See, that's what I mean,
screw up the end game, nothing else matters."

But what about _____?

I do not know what word to put in that space. Happiness?

Yes. I am writing to ask whether you are happy.
I am writing to promise that what washes out to sea

winds up on some other beach, changed but vital,
        pulsing with difference.

The Journalist in Love

In the last moments before plagiarism
when all thoughts remain your own

she is the lightning that blurs:
tulip-shaped birthmark, flame tattoo,

open mouth. Your favorite
pastime was always the hanging

of a scoundrel on a gallows of his own words—
you learned to hide your drawl, your scars, your ingrown nails.

Asking questions is the easy part.
There's the job and there's the burying,

deep below the red dirt of your childhood.
When thunderheads whip oak trees into frenzy

you recognize yourself in the thrashing leaves—
storm pitchforks, language fails and all you have left

is the desperation you were born with.
Her name. The echo. The ranting sky. The echo.

The Bank Robber in Love

This bedroom offers temporary refuge. Imagine
these curtains rising on last stand, blaze of glory, the flames

in which we'll go down on each other. There is no escape plan.
Clowns rise in the path like paragraphs. My fate

is riddled with rivers: placid, polluted, problematic.
Winter nears, figments begin to freeze. I have faked my way

through every questionnaire, through one orgasm
after another. I am stud horse and stopgap.

I refuse to be profound, and our affair may be pinned
between trance and virginity but we're not dead yet.

Hide me, help me, take my bullet. Everything you've heard is a lie.

The Governor in Love

We snorkel in your depths, we lace like coral—
we wait for the paperback. Your arm muscles rope & rhyme,

unsolved collision of flesh. Seagulls soundtrack
our imagination, this beach, this canyon cottage

with pine-cone lawn, shadow-splotched, greenlit.
All we ask is movie sex, waxmelt, math problem,

bubbling highway—this heat. Umbrella my plants,
our terra cotta plans, your wind-scattered genius—

it is fire hazard, feast, the long flight home.

The Bartender in Love

The things we do for luck: stopping by the drugstore for a bag of pink
        razors
after another uneventful episode pouring hardluck drinks

for those seeking forgiveness, or permission:
beerspill, sweatstain, stale tobacco, uneasy glances

at my elbow tattoos. Breathe in this polluted sweep—
what passes for fresh air. My city, my time of night,

my shortcuts & streetlights. We've all done these scenes:
cat knocks over trash can & our hero relaxes

thinking danger past. We've all fallen in love
with the same three stars: those bright enough

to shove through the haze. One day I awoke
& it had been a long time since I'd told

my favorite jokes, you know, women
& batteries, foxes & elephants—not even

faintly amusing anymore & anyone who thinks
people don't change hasn't seen my bald spot.

I am a long way from sleep: neon storefront, all-hours pharmacy,
at home a woman who cares enough to shave her legs,

& something resembling ordinary
burbling through the cracks in the sidewalks.

In the distance a siren. Another possibility unfolding.

Self-Portrait as a Vampire Trying to Read *Twilight* on a Cross-Country Flight

First: a continent of rain. Clouds bruise belly of shimmying jet. Knuckles whiten. Words blur, focus impossible. Every story gets it wrong about you: there's little shame in fear of dying. It's the living that slices and crawls and undoes. The couple across the aisle battle *The New York Times* crossword. This is not a project two people should do together, at least not out loud—innermost uncertainties air, facts almost remembered from sixth grade. "An emu is a bird?" "Could that be 'melee'? Scene of a great disturbance?" "No I think it's 'squall.'" Two hours in and they've filled less than a third of the puzzle. "What could 'feverish' be if there's a B here and an I there?" Who are these people? How did they end up together? What draws them to each other, to word games they have no talent for? Was it sex? The taste of blood? This book, this sealed air, this eternal headache. The plane ratchets from side to side. Pulses quicken, backs straighten. Whisper: *Burning, my darlings, burning.*

Love Poem Totally About Wallpaper and Not at All About Something Else, Like Breasts

First thing you learn as a grown-up is no one likes wallpaper someone else picked out. I know something about thistles, too, and no one wants to see your leftover thistles on the walls of their sunny goddamn happy-ever-after kitchens. Not even if you include the Latin names. Not even in pretty fruit-gum stripes. I could tell you about her breasts. Other body parts, too. You don't want to hear it. When a guy's alone in a hotel room longing for contact, it doesn't matter how good a quarterback he used to be, he's just another jerk with his cock in his hand. I can't help it, you should see these thistles. They're ridiculous. I know you don't believe me.

Hyperglycemia

The bartender brings drinks I did not order and tells me she used to dance under the name Kandi Cigarettes. Fake ashes and the taste of chalk, the hunger of strangers. She says she learned more about human nature than she cares to repeat, more about desire, about emptiness. She says she did this trick on stage with Mentos and a two-liter of Diet Coke. She says the symbolism was obvious but the money was good. When she bends over for ice, her shirt pulls up. The tattoo on the small of her back is maybe a rose. Maybe a dragon. She says, "Try this one, it tastes just like a Snickers." She says, "You should have seen the ending, it was something." She says, "*I* was something," and she's looking past me, at some idea of herself that she can't quite see, that maybe no one has seen, and I'm thinking about her skin all wet and slick and saccharine, and I'm drinking this drink, and this drink is so sweet my teeth hurt. She is right about how it tastes. She is right about everything.

The *New York Post* Runs a Photo of a Man About to Be Killed by a Subway Train and Everyone on the Internet Looks at It

Thank goodness our living rooms are immaculate—no shame
in keeping plastic sheeting over the good love seat

until the pastor comes by, of course it's no trouble
to put on tea and talk about the new neighbors,

moved from just such a place: where a man could fall
or be pushed into the path of a train,

but they seem like they'll fit in here. Our motto is "Wait Your Turn,"
our motto is "Keep Your Shit to Yourself,"

our motto is "We Know the Lyrics to Many Lovely Songs."
We like our mysteries solved within the hour

and our cornbread served without punctuation—
we are skeptical of so much flavor and well aware

when condescended to. We teach our children
that it's not blood or bone but hope that hurts. So forgive us

when we close our laptops and exit the room
to rake the season's last leaves into the street

and take the retriever for a walk in the evaporating light,
let us erase this image from ourselves and erase

ourselves from this image until they are all that remains:
the man who sees what's coming,

another man with no way to stop,
the photographer's flash—pitiful, distant star.

Love Poem During the Opening Scenes of *Law & Order*

Give me a body in the first ninety seconds
& I'll give you an hour, my life, my heart—
give me your mouth, your mouthing,
pale O of your secrets, harmonic vibration
of knife on sidewalk-stain. Crack wise
about death & I swoon in your vines.
The best surprises: those we see coming:
tooth in trash can, severed metaphors
ballooning from smokestacks. Give voice
to our yellowed marriage. Kiss me
in a rising elevator & we'll both pretend
to be shocked by what we find
dripping from this vigilant ceiling.
If I recognize your tattoo
you become my prime suspect,
if I taste wine on your tongue,
if you've done something with your hair.
Misdirection's the only direction
& we all want more face time.
You have thirty minutes to catch me,
I have thirty more to slip away—
trickster, guest star, comely associate,
you survive sarcasm & passion,
devotion & disregard. Come, walk with me
around this corner, we will stumble
into & out of someone else's plot.
Here: the flesh we were expecting,
the roles we were born to play.

LOOKING FOR LOVE ON ALL THE WRONG REALITY SHOWS

Ha Ha Ha Thump

It all starts with a cake taped down in the trunk of a Buick,
chalk outline of your ex-boyfriend
on the floor of our bedroom,

he was a Promise Keeper, god-fearer, secret masturbator,
it was never going to work between you,

not like the extravagant promises we've made:
You read *To Kill a Mockingbird* in the other room
while I highlight whole chapters of *Gatsby*,

except the parts about water, about distance,
the parts that imply some understanding has been reached.

Turn off the lights, my darling.
You be Angelina, Julia, Jennifer or the other Jennifer,
I'll be Brad or Ben or whoever—
one of us does the dishes, the other scoops the cat pans,

we'll vacuum and dust until morning
in our new-fangled, old-fashioned,

pineapple-upside-down Hollywood marriage.

The Poet & the Supermodel

(A Rearranged Marriage)

LIKE HUMID

The rain and the rain and the wind won't stop.
We cancel our picnic plans to sit on opposite ends
of the couch and tweet our small arguments to the world—

I have to remind Heidi not to bring the judging home,
the children are not contestants,
her affection not a prize to be earned,

we should all have permanent immunity.
She cocks her eyebrow, says (again, again),
"One day you're in, the next day you're out,"

a joke exactly as funny as the first time she used it.
I answer, as I always do, that that I mate for life,
she won't get out of *this* marriage so easily

and we both spend some time wondering
about this saltwater we've fallen into.
Her face is on TV selling something neither of us wants.

"Let's go upstairs and fool around," one of us says.
"The kids will be home any minute," the other one says.
Each of us disappears into the other's vague disappointment.

Heidi says, "I brought you something,"
and it's another shirt I hate. At some point
I should be honest about desire

but I cannot put the words in any order
that makes as much sense as the shape that lingers in the air
when she walks into or out of a room.

I HUED MILK

Relationships are anagrams of other relationships,
as poems reassemble what was written before—
Heidi understands this before I do. "What are
you writing?" she asks. "Letter to a friend,"
I say, and hide my paper. The weather
has nothing to do with what's happening inside
but it's an easy mistake. Left untouched, flesh cools
to the temperature of the air around us.
Like anything. Heidi knows me better
than I know myself. She is making coffee cake
from a box mix, the house
smells of cinnamon and sugar,
artificial preservatives and easy sentiment.
I would rather be fed than asked if I am hungry.

DUE HIM ILK

Not everything needs to be written—
Heidi's most withering insult.
Written by me, she means.

Even now she waits in our bed
and I cannot bring myself
to go upstairs. The body

is the origin of meaning,
the root of all language.
When I discover a word

that has evolved to mean
its exact opposite
I imagine that word

tattooed on her side—
ink that never spills,
rose that never dulls.

KID HELIUM

Heidi drinks more wine, tries to explain
the rubber hand illusion. She is supposed to be
at work, taping B roll in the park before the rain
but this is better. She splays her fingers
and asks me to use my imagination.
She has no idea what I dream about.
She pretends I gave her those rings
though we both know better. This mood
is light, easy, a floating balloon.
But I am careful to avoid sudden movements,
not to overcommit. If the flesh is being touched
the mind can ignore anything. "There is no loss
a body can't get used to," Heidi says. "Nothing
we can't live without." She's trying to tell me something
about the importance of feeling. But what I hear
is there's no hammer that won't make us flinch.

This Is <u>Not</u> a Love Poem for April from *Teenage Mutant Ninja Turtles*

This is the hiss of steam from an elaborate sewer system
in a city of rooftops and perpetual nighttime—

this is our love affair evaporating from under our feet.
We are essentially alone anyway, but it has been nice

to pretend otherwise. There's a reason seeing yellow
makes an electric fence of my skin, makes my mouth wet.

There's a reason you've started screening my calls,
a reason they'll cast a renowned beauty in the movie version.

O reboot! So much starting over, it's difficult
for anyone around you. I am not your father,

your brother, your super-villain ex-boyfriend,
but you will never stop expecting so little from me,

never stop looking elsewhere when you need
to be rescued. This is not a love poem.

This is not an apology. This is not the threat
that looms over our humanity. Your investigation

continues. You research and program and maybe
learn martial arts, maybe you and your friends

will save the world, but there's little room for me.
There's nothing I can do about the warmth of my blood.

Self-Portrait as Riker to Troi

My darling, my alien, my thorn bush with the red berries, my shipwreck, my island, my midnight, I have run out of excuses not to write you.

I thought to ask how long you will wait, but what if you are not waiting?

Let me go home. Come with me.

Let me show you mountaintop and snowfall, let us crack the shell of the far-off sky. I'll show you my planet, you show me yours. I weary of traveling alone. Which secrets will most surprise you? Surely you sense the depth of my hunger.

You always have been a better bluffer than anyone knows. What if the answer to my questions is more questions?

O my ambition, my cowardice, my earthquake, my fear and folly and fantasy, you have seen my favorite mistakes, anticipated my best guesses, outlasted my anger. Every journey ends the same way.

If this letter is all we have then let us read and read. Let the rising sun keep us awake.

Beyond these stars, more stars, and more, and more.

Let us accelerate. Let us blur and burn.

Love Poem for a Short-Lived Television Show

The Wrecking Crew, ABC, Fall 1991

Even the best hour has no room for comedy *and* drama. Not choosing is the mistake that cannot be forgiven. Once it's too late, it's easy to blame time. To say you expected more than four episodes to put the world in order. But there always was only one possible ending. You knew this. The way Dan knew the first time he looked at Denise, the whole of their love story arcing before him even though she was engaged to Brett. The way we all knew, because Brett was a special guest and only stars fall in love. The way Julio knew he never was going to fix those dents in his truck. The way Crazy Teddy and Happy knew their friendship mattered more than the bickering and eventually they would have a chance to prove it. The way the chess board on that stack of old tires was a metaphor: no one knew who else was playing but someone kept making all the right moves. Those stranded strangers in this crowded but inevitably lonely city, their flat tires and fender-benders, their drained batteries and hissing radiators. And you, all of you, with your straight teeth and imitation bodies and blue jumpsuits with the perfect grease stains and the talking parrot in the garage who always got the hour's last line. If any of it sounds too easy, it's because time is a kind of geography. Imagine it: a map, a truck, a destination. Imagine someone waiting. Imagine someone who needs you.

The Pope Imagines Life as a Married Man

Whoever falls asleep first keeps
the other awake. Whoever sings
is off-key. Whoever rises last
makes the bed. The toothpaste
is less of an issue than I expected.

Worse to argue or to be heard arguing,
this is the heart of every disagreement—
you do not like it when I disrobe
before the half-open window, the raised shades.
"There is no one out there," I say.
I say, "No one cares," You say,
"I care, isn't that enough?"

Under the weight of this ring
I cannot grip a pen
but if I wrote you a note
it would be about sex:
50 *Shades of Holy Shit That Felt Good.*

I imagine the smell of forsythia
and saltwater, the sound of the ocean
in the neighbors' mower,
the splashed light of passing cars.
Perhaps I have gotten some details
wrong but no one's infallible
in this house. My back

aches more each morning
but my body and my blood
will never grow weary
of your mouth
making the shape of my name.

The Night Before His Wedding, the Famous Golfer Takes a Stripper to Tour the Construction Site of a Course That Will Bear His Name

Consider the earthmoving—
these machines not in use,
looming empty nightsky skeletons.

Everyone is fungible
except me. Everyone
thinks this but for me

it is true. This robust furrow,
red-dirt trench
in land that used to have

purpose: to sustain, to offer meaning
beyond pleasure. But pleasure
is why we are here

so when I call you Diamond
or Dallas or whatever,
your made-up name

only adds to the lies
I've told merely tonight:
I've never been lost.

We have an understanding.
She doesn't love me.
I want you. Such lack

of originality—it's an act,
like your writhing.
I like to see how much credit

being me earns me.
Itch, scratch, collapse.
My faith is portable,

my life is the final hole
of a bad round:
swing, swing, swing, putt,

none of it matters
except that everyone's watching.
I'm bored already

yet my body is happy
to go through the motions,
this rehearsed dissonance.

I should apologize
but my tissue is failing,
stitches separating,

unwiring, unsparking,
powder damp.
Spike and wane,

the yellow flare—
grass grows wet
underneath our spent flesh,

here, where the sixteenth hole will be:
over a pond, after a hard dogleg left
around the shell

of the old barn
repainted, left standing
as reminder

of our power over structure.
Imagine topography transformed.
Imagine the scars left by bulldozers.

Mick Jagger's Penis Turns 69

Mick Jagger's penis is pleased to meet you.
Mick Jagger's penis is the John Lennon's penis
of penises. Also, the Steven Tyler scarf collection
of penises, the David Lee Roth midair crotch thrust,
the Gene Simmons codpiece, the Axl Rose attitude of penises.
This is a lot of pressure for a penis,
big shoes for a penis to fill. Mick Jagger's penis
doesn't ask for much, these days. Mick Jagger's penis
is strongly influenced by the blues and knows
whom this song is about. There are two versions
of Mick Jagger's penis: the one the world sees
and the one that lies awake at night
and worries it has let someone down.
Sometimes it wants to be remembered,
to leave its mark on the world, it wants
to be more than footnote, punchline, punching bag.
Sometimes it just wants to be held.
It grows weary of everything having two meanings.
If you ask Mick Jagger's penis about its dreams,
it will tell you about a certain lightning storm
over a certain lake—which means
nothing more or nothing less than what it was:
the dark water, the sky splitting open.

Self-Portrait as Han to Leia, on Hoth

Another planet battle-scored & near-exterminated:
      we crave this cave-chase & escape plan,
our evacuation inevitable. We have always been
      outnumbered & every system is remote

from somewhere. Our future pendulums away from us,
      our small stars extinguish each other
in the heart's dark sky. You are not afraid.
      An empire grows in my chest. Pistol me open,

let my rebellious ribs steam into the frost,
      feed on the warmth of me. We cannot destroy
all that threatens us & ice will not slake
      your salted tongue. Given flame, we choose to burn.

Self-Portrait as Nicolas Cage and John Travolta
in *Face/Off*

I try to be the man you hunger for. I try to imagine
how my face looks refracted in your eyes—
imagine sharing skin. Imagine muscles,
posture, voice. Love means transformation
means struggle means vendetta.
We wake nose to nose and pretend
we don't mind each other's breath.
We stay up all night trying
to think of something new to try.
I thought I was the hero pretending to be the villain
but maybe it's the other way around?
Marriage is an action-adventure,
a thriller, a mystery: plot-driven,
fast-paced, predictable, overflowing
with unnecessary violence.
Our story doesn't stand up to scrutiny:
too many other people involved,
too many obstacles to overcome.
No one would ever believe it
but it turns out belief doesn't count.
All that matters is forward momentum.
I cannot remember when I stopped
thinking of my body as my own,
I wonder if you intend to return it.
It does not matter how much damage
happens along the way—
the ending will be happy if we tell ourselves it's happy.

WHAT HAPPENS AT THE BLOCK PARTY STAYS AT THE BLOCK PARTY

Ha Ha Ha Thump

We are the men at this block party, we are naked
as beer bottles, we are the aging rock songs

that bleed like smoke or gravel. We gaze with lost eyes
at our wives, their legs. Our children are pale streaks, tiny fires

at the edge of our vision. We are keepers of a ghost ship
here in the early twenty-first century in America:

this time and place reserved precisely for us. Our veins
rope and pulse and promise extravagantly, give voice

to the dangers swimming in our insubstantial bodies.
We are broken window, insurance fraud, loophole, privilege,

we are the syncopation of weather and family.
The moon unmoors. We drift toward its yawn.

We are, each of us, a clown with a heart condition.

Nocturne at the Grill

I do this impression of myself,
only not so funny—
husband, father, provider—
overcooking meat for my family,
charring the remains of a chicken or two
because I too am bitter I cannot fly.
Take that, flight! Take this, flame!
Take that, once-living creature
whose severed muscle has become my meal!
Everything I do, I do less well
than my grandfathers would have.
I regret the mounds of junk in my garage,
the crusted floorboards of my dented car,
my toolboxes full of bent nails and drywall dust,
takes me thirty minutes to find a screwdriver
and then I'm unsure what to do with it.
Something about twisting, tightening,
firming up the loose or leaky connections
of my life. Probably
I should be a vegetarian
but my heart would miss the blood
or so I tell myself,
and here I am thinking of you reaching for me
after the children go to bed,
thinking of your flesh and form
and the heat between bodies—
fire that cannot be contained in a metal box,
not even this very fancy one of chrome and black
which we picked out together at Lowe's
or maybe it was Target.

Chapter That Rushes Through the Backstory

We marry in a town called Hairspray, called Collapsing Star,
      called I Want You in the Worst Way,
in the Chapel of Our Lady Who Jumped into the Waterfall.

We drink to the health of our boundless potential.

We buy a starter home curved like your inner thighs,
we plant somber flowers along the drive,

we spend many hours baking elaborate pastries—
we become our favorite neighbors' favorite neighbors.

These stories are never easy to tell,
titles do not reconcile with content,

endings are easy to predict. You say, "This all feels
      so familiar."
You say, "Lift me from this sleep."

Elegy for the Summer Games

I used to be thinner.
On my shelf a collection of trophies
I did not win.
I could keep them balanced on my stomach.
When games are played
often I am elected to keep score.
Something to do with counting,
wanting, trust.
All this tallying up.
This reckoning.
I read a poem about football
but I wanted it to be about swimming.
Splash. Immersion. Crave.
To give oneself completely
to water.
For maximum speed
one must hold one's fingers
a precise distance apart—
the effect of a web.
To move without encumbrance
is to stay alive.
Nothing is ever easy,
which is why it matters so much.
It's not the metal we find precious.
I miss being touched that way—
triumphantly—
first lips, then teeth, testing for the give.

Your Marriage Gets Louder as You Get Older

Everything begins as whisper, tiptoe, feather in night air: predator you never hear dropping from sky. Then faint clatter of dishes in faraway kitchen, hush of half-muted crime drama, soap opera, self-contained narrative. Argument between neighbors, voices rising from behind locked doors on a block where such things are frowned upon. Traffic from two streets over. Distant train whistles. The rising siren of someone else's trauma. The muffled bang: perhaps gunshot, perhaps backfire. Safe, still, to ignore. To pretend away. To slip between the folds of your own dreams like a roommate's alarm clock. Things change without your paying attention. One week the construction site is a mile away, then four blocks, then trucks are backing down your driveway. That baby crying is in your arms. The life-flight helicopter is landing in your front yard. The roaring is in your ears, your skin, your heart. It is the sound of a drowning ocean. It is what you have been waiting for.

Chapter in Which We Place Great Faith in the Word "Temporary"

If I asked for a reason to stay awake
would you touch my eyelids
with the tips of your fingers,
tell me a story about making love in the woods?
Your skin smells of new soap,
artisanal, all woodsmoke and moss
and expensive. We cannot fake
this moment. Rain's coming,
we can feel a thickening in the air,
and spring not far behind,
the night already almost warm enough
to leave the windows open
except our alcoholic neighbor
has left his radio on again,
blaring postgame commentary
or political analysis—some kind of hum
and babble, maddening. Last summer
we found ourselves at the Missouri State Fair,
got matching airbrush tattoos—
skull-and-crossbones
because it seemed out of character
and we felt so out of place. It's sad,
the thing with our neighbor,
and his house and yard are going to shit—
he has lined his driveway
with trash cans of rainwater
surrounding his fancy foreign SUV
which has four flat tires for months now
because, we all assume, his license
has been revoked. There's only so much
we can do, which sounds like a copout
but it's mostly just the truth.

When I was twenty I was an arrogant fuck
and consoled myself by assuming
no one else had any imagination
or aspiration. Probably
I haven't changed all that much.
I want you. I am also tired.
This is where my life has led.
I am going to close my eyes now
and wait for you to touch me.

Self-Portrait as Punxsutawney Phil

In which I bring on six more weeks of winter by carrying the salt and shovels to the garage. In which I bring on six more weeks of marriage by washing the storm windows. In which I cause a block-wide fire by spray-painting my name on the stop sign at the top of the street. In which I bring down the stars by wishing too many times for the wrong things. In which I dream about your lips. In which the ground splits open. In which the flood fails to cleanse. In which we learn to hunt. In which I shoot an arrow through the eye of the alphabet and invent language. In which many of the words fall into place.

Nocturne in Which We Fail Yet Again to Have Sex in Your Parents' Hot Tub

Your breasts at the surface of the roiling water. The smell of chlorine
and desire. We divide and assign the space between us.

My specialty is keeping score, yours is pretending not to.
We are not supposed to stay in water this hot

more than 15 minutes. Plenty of time to pretend
we could not drown here or anywhere

in the middle of our own lives. Three walls away
our children dream of life without us,

your parents sleep with their television on. One of us
slides closer. One of us places a finger in the other's mouth,

one of us stands, dripping, to reach for a towel.
The tub's motor falls quiet. The air suddenly cold

against overheated skin. Absence swells to the shape of absence,
water closes in over the holes our bodies once filled.

Stick Figures in Love

Lying naked on this bed in the cold sunshine of afternoon is the closest we come to honesty. Don't even ask about the sex. All angles & awkward juxtapose. The slow end of the day, the bitter-chalk taste of hardboiled yolk. We feast on made-up memories, we never say what we mean. Seen from above, our shadows would resemble dancers: swell & spin & rise & thaw & somehow, somehow beautiful.

She Blinded Me With Molecular Nanotechnology

First thing in the morning, we're already
trying on hats, scrubbing away at smeared selves.
Size matters, but not the way you think.
Mirror steams. We finger-scrawl messages
in this fog, think ourselves original. I shave.
She showers and provides perspective:
a nanometer is the length my beard grows
in the time it takes to lift razor from sink to skin.
Even the smallest spot of blood holds all our secrets,
those lies I've told or thought or lived
staining this tear-away tissue against my neck,
the deaths I've beaten and the one I won't
enmeshed in that fragile twisted code:
think of the stories this blade could tell.
To answer questions before they are asked—
this is marriage, or science, or close enough. We think
we are permanent but that's only temporary.
Hurricane's coming. The ocean's a mess,
those who care already putting value to damage.
We are not insured against flood.
Someone launches invisible wires into the storm
to measure the strength of impossible,
the color of wind. The more we know
the more we know. If you can collect the wires after
you can rule the world. We collapse
into bed, we mouth and skin and savor
and pretend our touching has purpose.
We passive each other's aggressive
and call it communication. We are without
power for days, we are not alone,
we are still wobbly from last week's earthquake
which we never saw coming. Tomorrow

remains our blind spot but we're working on it.
Married four years and I still don't understand
what she does when she's somewhere else
or the way her mind moves even when she tells me
the key is finding atoms of similar size and stickiness.
This is the future. This is fiction.
This is the world's smallest electrical motor,
controlled by chemists at 450 degrees below zero,
rotating in a way that is not random. Hey,
it's something. It's vanishing point and given day
and the discovery that makes possible
a new kind of miracle. This is proper noun,
payday, pitfall. We need a special microscope
to talk to each other anymore. We're still trying
to replicate the subatomic sophistication
of a potato. We scan and tunnel
and every system leads to another until there is no
molecule we cannot create from scratch.
Ten years ago we thought we were ten years
from having enough tiny robots
to live happily ever after. Maybe
nothing has changed, maybe everything.
Imagine the heart that heals itself.

Self-Portrait as My Grandparents at Dusk, Bon Secour Beach

So many waves are born out beyond our complaints.
Stairs rise from this sand toward laboring stars and a city

that promises to hold us for the night. You're asking
what it means but it's easier to say nothing.

To imagine a different gulf. A different comma
of twilight curling dark gold above our heads,

different gulls disappearing from a different sky—
it's all silhouette and contrast anyway. Young men

nearby laugh and break glass, thump their heart-cages in time
to the music that tumbles from Novas and Chargers:

such astounding certainty in those shining metal shapes.
Once we were so good with our hands. Let us

say we do live forever. Say our sons and our sons' sons
have gathered to sing and we have come to listen.

The sand is cold. The water is clear. Your hands are cold.
You have trouble breathing. We invented this landscape

out of language and hope and hunger. Say our daughters
carry our silence with them as they board that boat

already pitching into darkness. Say they send
a bottle of flames back through the salt. Who are we

to be afraid? We may not be given the ending we desire.
There is no ending. Still, we must kneel. Must ask.

WHAT GOES
"HA HA HA THUMP"?

Ha Ha Ha Thump

Puppy love, guppy love, hippy-dippy
get-high-in-the-driveway love—
let's wait until the house is empty,

you can wriggle out of your bellbottoms
and tie me to the posts of your parents' bed
with your dad's wide paisley ties. Let's pretend

we know what to do with the vast acres
of time between us and the horizon,
we are not too young to taste the difference

between savannah and oasis,
between mirage and miracle. Look!
Something has spooked the gazelle:

an elephant shambling across the wrong continent,
a macaw calling someone else's name,
a hyena falling out of a tree.

Nocturne: Orgasms at Nineteen

Never did know what the hell we were doing. Still
don't, all these years later and no more insight

than those earliest sweaty nights with most of our clothes on.
So much humidity, terrible for hair and makeup,

our disguises melting away, our difficulty breathing
or even walking at the same pace. Insomnia,

motion sensors, the neighbor's dog who never stopped barking,
my fingers inside you on the back porch.

You know why they call it *le petit mort*? Has nothing

to do with ecstasy or transcendence.
It's this that's like death: if it never happened

we would not know when to stop. Art requires
beginning and end—

between there somewhere
we hold each other for as many nights as we can steal.

In Lieu of Apology

I can offer you the heat shimmer off Highway 11 in deep July, the smell of melting tar, the only way out of town.

I can offer my hand on a walk around the lake. I can offer the dying grass, the dry wind, the taste of grape bubble gum and everything that mattered in my childhood.

I can offer stumble, spit-take, outcast, skinned knuckles, dirty knees.

I can offer hair-metal ballads on speakers I installed myself in my Civic: sap and sadness and shiny guitars.

I can offer you six years of escape plans.

I wake. I rise. I fill my arms and search for you. I am lost. I can offer you my state of being lost. I can offer a mouthful of sand and all the words I have not yet formed.

Chapter in Which the Issue of My Salvation Becomes a Problem

Everything I have read about rivers is wrong.

She asks me to get on my knees beside her.
I do not know how. Would not know where to begin.

She says, "I think I am dying." We all are.
She asks for something I cannot give. Will not give.

I once thought there was no line I would not cross

but her prayer is the point where the river empties
into Lake Michigan. The same river every time.

The same music, the same making love, the same
heron taking flight from beneath the same silver maple.

Venus' Navel

1.

The first act of the world opens on you, uncovered under a ceiling fan. It is too warm to sleep, too late to be awake. We are so, so far from home. You complain when I become too familiar. You want a stranger's touch. You want the slow curve back to where we began.

2.

The story goes that the innkeeper caught a glimpse of the goddess undressed and was inspired to craft sustenance in her image. There are other stories. Murder, intrigue, a woman in translucent red. At the window, I watch—the only role I dare claim for myself.

3.

You say, sometimes fog is good. You say, there's no such thing as wishful thinking. The shape of a fortune cookie is not a coincidence. The fortune inside suggests the only unforgivable sin is a missed opportunity. There's more than one reasonable interpretation.

Nocturne: On Language

A most audacious lie: we've agreed to pretend we understand each
      other.

Such arrangement is the reason no one ever served Dali
the boiled telephone he craved in place of the lobster he ordered.

We do not know what happens when the heart catches up to the
      tongue.

This is not an aberration, there are no aberrations,
the body knows what it wants.

Nocturne with Poor Decisions

That time, say, you shoved me against the wall
and we pretended we liked things rough.

We don't have to live in separate states
to call it a long-distance relationship. We don't

write, don't call, we get lost in the hazy outlines
of our own front porch at dusk. I drink tequila

from your lips, swim buzzingly
through the tangle and mystery of your hair,

I can't tell which wounds are happening,
have happened, could happen.

We have differing tastes in music
though I'll listen to anything

if it gets you to open your mouth.
Let's say I stand, stumble. Let's say

fall. Say *follow* and *fire*. Say we end up
in the crawlspace, brushing away spiderwebs,

our knees on stones and broken glass.
You strike the match. I touch flame to fuse.

Origami Figures in Winter

The petals, the stalk.
The frozen ground,
the hectic silk.

To celebrate
our anniversary
we're circulating

in this weird museum
of tiny paper landscapes:
you carpe, I'll diem,

let's make believe
anyone could do this—
the sculpt and crease

and flapping bird,
the mountains, valleys,
pleats, reverses

and stellated icosahedrons:
these thin little nothings
do go on and on.

We are missing verbs.
Sometimes scissors,
always swerve—

the quickened heart,
our younger selves
back to where we started,

doing laundry in the cold:
the boy fluffs,
the girl folds.

Nocturne with Shovel & Storm

I imagine burying a jar of pennies until they turn green. In the middle of the coins an unwritten letter, sealed in an envelope, turning to dust.

The night spits back my shortcomings: my lack of follow-through, all I leave unspoken.

The stars flash like bone & vanish into the clouds. I feel most at home when lost like this.

The trees crack in the wind. The rain begins slowly, gains strength, sluices & plumes. Dirt to mud. The washing away. The unburying of certain promises.

This woman I love, I imagine her waiting for the lightning to see me clearly: I am silhouette, shadow, splintered limb.

Love Poem for Saturday's Apocalypse

Say we get a room upstairs. Say we spend
the next 36 hours silk-tangled, heat-flustered,

forgiven for all our skin. Say your flesh
quenches my last thirst. Say my fingers

are the rapture you believe in. Still,
we will have regrets. Say things go dust to ashes

or whatever. If we wake up together Sunday
come loot with me. Give me your mouth.

Say my name. Keep my world alive.

HOW A STORY ENDS
IS HOW WE WILL
REMEMBER IT

Ha Ha Ha Thump

We're finding our way south along this Midwestern interstate,
extravagant concrete river twisting through thunderheads—

we are the movie version of ourselves,

all simultaneous orgasm and fuzzy-dog joke,
bravado in the face of mortality. Strobe-lit corn fields

stretch as far as we can see, clouds
dark as anvils unzip and singe the sky

of our marriage. This road trip

is nocturne, love poem, self-portrait,
rescue mission, last chance—

what if it's the storm sustaining us?
Uncertainty is not as funny as it used to be.

What we're looking for is form:

a sense of the proper order of things:
first lightning then thunder—

laughter to measure the silence between.

Chapter with the Power out After a Storm

There's no place open to eat. What if instead we start with the cancer?
That's ridiculous. No one does that.

The sky is like looking at the bottom of a river. Everything is interrupted.
Even the stones cannot hold still. You adjust the radio

looking for classic rock. Familiar but with an edge.

We drive beyond the city limits without planning to. We drive
across the long bridge. Bob Seger sings us farther from home,

Tom Petty, Stevie Nicks. It's perfect. It keeps us from having to talk.

Eventually we stop and share a six-pack under a lightning-striped maple.
The beer is warm.

The grass, in waves. The music. Another kind of weather.

The Ethnomusicologist & the Blackfoot Chief

The dark vowels of your eyes crave & curl
& say only nothing, only everything.
I catch myself expecting the sky

to walk in & spill your secrets. Perhaps
I never was supposed to fall in love
but your face is prairie upon which gold lingers

& the mood of this place is hopeful:
irresistible smell of hot ashes
& disappearing weather.

There is dirt on the hem of my sensible skirt.
To write, to celebrate, to predict.
To interpret means to condescend—

forgive me. All I ask
is the sharing: the wheatgrass, the forget-me-not.
From a certain angle, history

is mutable as wax cylinder,
miraculous as box camera—
this transcription of light & song.

Scientists Say One Language Disappears Every 14 Days

National Geographic, July 2012

The gin and tonic on your breath—
                                        so much is lost
to evaporation, translation, replication, the movie version:

these processes that occur only on the surface of a body.

There are cycles we control and those we cannot. Sounds
we make and sounds no one will ever make again.

It's goddamn hard just to talk to each other
                        some days. To say
only what you want, to give voice to desire: it seems the most basic

purpose of language. Yet it is the thing that escapes,
the warm air that rises.

Seven thousand tongues in the world and all I can think about is yours.

Can We Smell With Our Hearts?

Popular Science, April 2013

How long do I have to go without talking
before you stop listening?

I post personal ads on telephone poles:
Blue Belgian Bearded D'Anvers Cockerel

seeks life partner, height-weight-proportional please.
I have never felt so human. I have never felt

so dangerous. It turns out robots already
work side by side with us in rescue situations,

which of course is always
because when do we not need rescuing?

I imagine myself as a particular blood cell
with a specific role to play—

without olfactory information
I would swim in circles.

Suppose you had gone to Mississippi
for no particular reason: how long

before I thought to look in Hattiesburg?
How lonely I must appear.

How the Ocean Exhales

Nature, March 2013

I imagine, as I say goodnight and drive away,
the couple left on the sidewalk glad at my parting,

pleased to find themselves alone—
though it never was or will be otherwise.

I imagine the turning toward, the embrace,
the first few drops of a new rainfall.

All circulation is a system: predictable, purposeful.

We are in a period of deglaciation,
deep-water masses are mutable,

and what sinks to the ocean floor
grows restless, releases

whatever it had trapped in shallower spaces.

I imagine again the couple: how she holds him—
how they raise their faces to the sky,

what falls, what rises.

The Mafia Hypothesis

We surprise ourselves with occasional small kindnesses.
We have long assumed that our every interaction
is motivated by threat.
Loss and desire, held together by spit.

The cowbird will destroy the nest of non-cooperative birds.
Birds adjust.
The strange egg
becomes familiar.
We can get used to anything—

if you make me another mimosa, I will drink
though I have bad memories of champagne.
The value of retaliation has always been the question.

When the season turns, we will gather enough twigs and scraps
to start all this again.

At the Whim of Human Fancy

We have accelerated the evolution of chickens:
this is one way to talk about progress. To look back
without nostalgia. Scientists suggest hens' newly yellow skin
has something to do with the ability to lay eggs year-round,
and so it always comes down to hunger. I don't know
why I don't write you more letters. I don't know
why in my dreams the desert seems to be a place of great mystery—
cactus and some sort of quest. I expect
you have stopped waiting by now. After so many
trips to any empty mailbox, even the sky
would fall out of love with the sand. Even if
we could start over, would we? I grew up
with chickens, did I tell you that? And goats
and the occasional pig. It was my job to feed them all.
I hated the responsibility. Of course
there's never one right way to do anything
but there are as many wrong ways as spines
on a saguaro. It's kind of genius, as painful
ways to spread seeds across the land go,
the barb on the needle that keeps it holding on.
It might sound like I'm talking about God,
but it could also mean I'm more trusting
than I used to be. Faith has nothing to do with it.
I can do just less than enough over and over,
I can fall short and shorter. The chickens
are wider, more productive, more agreeable.
All this within a handful of generations.
I don't know what else you expect from me.

Last Two Speakers of Dying Language Refuse to Talk to Each Other

Time Magazine, April 2011

We try: communion with the dirt, the roots, the dead.
To molder. To wake. To rest our cheeks

against another's shoulder. Then everything breaks.
How the flesh arcs. How this charade.

We venture, plungingly. We limit, we flourish.
Neither of us is easily dismissed. Hush.

We hide dismay in liquid darkness—
to inch toward each other, our tongues

hostage to the remnants of betrayal.
Oh how we are directionless, unbedded, unlimbed.

Sex Lives of Certain Invertebrates

Too many jellyfish being born
means something's wrong with the narrative.
Don't mistake this for hierarchy
or judgment. It's the water, the salt,
the warming of rocks under the water.
Conditions are perfect but shouldn't be—
words need space to breathe.
Stories need what's left unsaid,
touching needs the part untouched.
It's in the contrast that meaning forms.
It's in the contact, the lack, the fertilization.
Float. Sink. Attach. Wait. Wait.
Release to float again. This is the cycle,
a balanced stack of fragile saucers yielding
to a translucent drifting reminder
of how the world works,
how things are muted underwater,
how we fall in love, how we
replicate our favorite mistakes.

The Visible Path of a Meteoroid Is Sometimes Called a Falling Star

Let's say it's about you. Say you see a meteor on your evening walk: bright green and lifting from somewhere far to somewhere farther, all forward momentum, rising action, narrative arc. You hold your husband's hand and pretend to make the same wish. Back at home, you tell the world of the beauty you have witnessed. Say your friends immediately like the update. Say you have trouble sleeping, say you dream of lilac bushes and maybe snowstorms, the Iowa kind: terrible fury and swirl, you need a clothesline to venture from house to barn without disappearing into the crush and cold and dark. Maybe a father did not make it home. Maybe a brother. The mystery remains, though you crave resolution. Even an unhappy ending is at least an ending. Say you write a new status. No one likes this one. Your friends are no longer online. When you look out the window, the meteor is not there, as you knew it would not be. Not green, but emptiness folding in on itself where green used to be. Hand over hand, the rope brittle in the wind.

Ars Poetica Disguised as a Love Poem Disguised as a Commemoration of the 166th Anniversary of the Rescue of the Donner Party

This is life: a series of difficult choices ending in death.
Along the way, try not to judge too harshly.

Share what you have, but not all of it.
Also, avoid shortcuts during winter months, or late fall,

lest your own late fall yield a new way of tasting the world—
limb and root, outcome and inspiration—

the height of the stumps reveals the depth of the snow
as the brightness now is equal to the blindness later,

as today will be rewritten tomorrow.
It's why we must keep moving.

Somewhere in the middle distance, an ocean
rises like a great column of light,

beckons like the salt and sweat of a first kiss.
This is why we carry on so. Knowing hunger

is but the first test. Like this. Only faster.
The season turns. The wind's slow sway,

the frostbite and flame, the infection creeping—
I thought myself too tired to go on.

Then you appeared, as if from California
or heaven, and held out your hand.

My ghost-bones stirred.
I let you in. You carried me out.

Acknowledgments

I am grateful to the editors of the journals where many of these poems first appeared, sometimes in different form or under different title:

Anti-: "Ha Ha Ha Thump ['The morning of the extravagant crime...']" and "The Bank Robber in Love"

The Bakery: "At the Midnight Garage Sale"

Baltimore Review: "Scientists Say One Language Disappears Every 14 Days"

Carolina Quarterly: "Ha Ha Ha Thump ['We are the men at this block party...']"

Cease, Cows: "Hyperglycemia" and "Love Poem for a Short-Lived Television Show"

The Cincinnati Review: "She Blinded Me with Molecular Nanotechnology"

The Dirty Napkin: "Self-Portrait as Punxsutawney Phil"

Eleven Eleven: "Sex Lives of Certain Invertebrates"

Four Way Review: "Self-Portrait as Han to Leia, on Hoth"

The Frank Martin Review: "Venus' Navel" and "The Breaking Point is the Coordinate on the Strain-Strength Curve at the Moment of Rupture"

FreezeRay: "This Is Not a Love Poem for April from *Teenage Mutant Ninja Turtles*" and "Self-Portrait as Nicolas Cage and John Travolta in *Face/Off*"

Gargoyle: "Love Poem During the Opening Scenes of *Law & Order*

The Georgetown Review: "Chapter in Which the Issue of My Salvation Becomes a Problem"

Grist: "Origami Figures in Winter"

Gulf Stream: "Nocturne at the Grill"

ILK Journal: "Elegy for the Summer Games"

JMWW: "The Bartender in Love"

The Journal: "Last Two Speakers of Dying Language Refuse to Talk to Each Other"

Menacing Hedge: "Due Him Ilk," "Kid Helium," "I Hued Milk," and "Like Humid"

The Minnesota Review: "The Governor in Love"

The Mondegreen: "Nocturne: Orgasms at Nineteen"

New Plains Review: "The Ethnomusicologist & the Blackfoot Chief"

PANK: "Self-Portrait as a Vampire Trying to Read *Twilight* on a Cross-Country Flight"

Posit: "In Lieu of Apology" and "At the Whim of Human Fancy"

Pretty Owl Poetry: "Nocturne: On Language" and "The Mafia Hypothesis"

Quarterly West: "The *New York Post* Runs a Photo of a Man About to Be Killed by a Subway Train and Everyone on the Internet Looks at It"

Rattle: "Mick Jagger's Penis Turns 69"

Ramshackle Review: "Stick Figures in Love," "Love Poem Totally About Wallpaper and Not at All About Something Else, Like Breasts," and "Your Marriage Gets Louder as You Get Older"

Revolution John: "The Journalist in Love"

RHINO: "Poem for Saturday's Apocalypse"

Rubbertop Review: "Chapter that Rushes Through the Backstory"

Stirring: "Chapter with the Power Out After a Storm"

Sundog Lit: "The Night Before His Wedding, the Famous Golfer Takes a Stripper to Tour the Construction Site of a Course That Will Bear His Name"

Sweet: "Nocturne with Poor Decisions"

Tahoma Literary Review: "Ars Poetica Disguised as a Love Poem Disguised as a Commemoration of the 166th Anniversary of the Rescue of the Donner Party"

TheThePoetry: "Nocturne in Which We Fail Yet Again to Have Sex in Your Parents' Hot Tub"

Toad the Journal: "Chapter in Which We Place Great Faith in the Word 'Temporary'"

Vinyl: "Nocturne with Shovel & Storm"

Waxwing: "How the Ocean Exhales," "Can We Smell with Our Hearts?" "Nocturne: Interrogation," and "Ha Ha Ha Thump ['We're finding our way south ...']"

"Mick Jagger's Penis Turns 69" was reprinted in *The Poetry of Sex* (Penguin UK). "Self-Portrait as Riker to Troi" appeared in *Make It So Again: Poetry Inspired by* Star Trek (Hyacinth Girl Press).

Notes

"Self-Portrait as Han to Leia, on Hoth" is after Dean Rader and Robert Frost; "Self-Portrait as Riker to Troi" is after Rader, but not Frost. "Elegy for the Summer Games" is after Mary Ruefle. "Like Humid," "Kid Helium," "Due Him Ilk" and "I Hued Milk" are after Kiki Petrosino's anagrammatic *Fort Red Border*. "Ars Poetica Disguised as a Love Poem Disguised as a Commemoration of the 166th Anniversary of the Rescue of the Donner Party" is after Matthew Olzmann. "The Ethnomusicologist & the Blackfoot Chief" is inspired by a photo of Frances Densmore, who was known as the song catcher, and the Blackfoot chief Mountain Chief.

About the Author

Amorak Huey, a longtime newspaper reporter and editor, now teaches writing at Grand Valley State University in Michigan. He is author of the poetry chapbook *The Insomniac Circus*, and his writing appears in *The Best American Poetry 2012*, *The Southern Review*, *Poet Lore*, *The Cincinnati Review*, *Quarterly West*, *Menacing Hedge*, *Rattle*, *Essay Daily*, and many other print and online publications.

OTHER SUNDRESS PUBLICATIONS TITLES

Stationed Near the Gateway, Margaret Bashaar
ISBN 978-1-939675-20-0 || $14.00

Till the Tide: An Anthology of Mermaid Poetry, Ed. Trista Edwards
ISBN 978-1-939675-14-9 || $18.00

Confluence, Sandra Marchetti
ISBN 978-1-939675-16-3 || $14.00

major characters in minor films, Kristy Bowen
ISBN 978-1-939675-19-4 || $14.00

Exodus in X Minor, Fox Frazier-Foley
ISBN 978-1-939675-18-7 || $10.00

Hallelujah for the Ghosties, Melanie Jordan
ISBN 978-1-939675-15-6 || $14.00

Fortress, Kristina Marie Darling
ISBN 978-1-939675-13-2 || $14.00

Not Somewhere Else But Here: A Contemporary Anthology of Women and Place,
Eds. Erin Elizabeth Smith, T.A. Noonan, Rhonda Lott, & Beth Couture
ISBN 978-1-939675-11-8 || $20.00

When I Wake It Will Be Forever, Virginia Smith Rice
ISBN 978-1-939675-10-1 || $14.00

A House of Many Windows, Donna Vorreyer
ISBN 978-1939675-05-7 || $14.00

The Hardship Post, Jehanne Dubrow
ISBN 978-1-939675-03-3 || $14.00

Too Animal, Not Enough Machine, Christine Jessica Margaret Reilly
ISBN 978-1-939675-02-6 || $10.00

Gathered: Contemporary Quaker Poets, Ed. Nick McRae
ISBN 978-1939675-01-9 || $15.00

One Perfect Bird, Letitia Trent
ISBN 0-9723224-8-5 || $14.00

The Bone Folders, T.A. Noonan
ISBN 0-9723224-6-9 || $14.00

CPSIA information can be obtained
at www.ICGtesting.com
Printed in the USA
FFOW05n0006170815

9 781939 675231